A 365 Journey of...
DISCOVERY, GROWTH, AND PERSONAL POWER

Dr. Mel Campbell

A 365 Journey of...
Discovery, Growth, and Personal Power

Dr. Mel Campbell

Circumference Press

Copyright © 2018 by
Published by Circumference Press

All rights reserved. This book may not be used or reproduced in any manner, in whole or in part, stored in a retrieval system or transmitted in any form (by electronic, mechanical, photocopied, recorded or other means) without written permission from the author, except as permitted by United States copyright law.

No liability is assumed with respect to the use of information contained herein. While every precaution has been taken in the preparation of this book, the author assumes no responsibility for errors or omissions. Neither is any liability assumed for damages resulting from the use of information contained herein.

ISBN: 978-1987794922

Cover art and design: Kimb Williams Graphic Design

Editing and layout by Jonathan Peters, PhD

Printed in the United States of America

I want to dedicate this book to my beautiful daughter, Willow.

I want to thank my best friend and partner, Ashley.

Finally, I want to give my appreciation to my Mother, Dad, and Brother for all the lessons you have taught me.

You're all amazing!

What you affirm becomes your reality!

Day 1

Day 2

I prepare for positive results!

Day 3

I feel like, and act like, a winner because I am a winner!

Day 4

I can get it done!

Day 5

Anything you don't feed, dies

and anything you feed, grows!

Day 6

Count Your Blessings!

Day 7

I take action and I get positive results!

Day 8

Meditation works and I use it today!

Day 9

Be still and have faith!

Day 10

Focus on your goals, rather than the negative!

Day 11

Be a doer who acts!

Day 12

Connect with your higher self

to get the results you want!

Day 13

Name it!
Claim it!

Day 14

Many people who are not alive today, would love to trade places with you!

Day 15

Every part of my life has purpose, has meaning, has hope!

Day 16

My inner strength is greater than any outer appearances!

Day 17

I am a fighter, ready for any challenge!

Day 18

I accept and adapt to change with confidence!

Day 19

I am enough!

Day 20

Today, be around people who lift you and lift others!

Day 21

Make the sacrifice for what you want!

Day 22

Tap into your power source!

Day 23

Use all your power to get things done!

Day 24

See the positive in all things today!

Day 25

I am 100% committed to make this happen!

Day 26

I let go any negative stories I am holding on to!

Day 27

I will not be lazy. I will get done what needs to be done!

Day 28

No matter what happens today, **I got this!**

Day 30

Use your positive mental attitude to get things done!

Day 31

I go after my goal today no matter what it takes!

Day 32

I am focused and powered up.

Let's go!

Day 33

I keep my head and

stay strong!

Day 34

I listen to my instinct!

Day 35

I am focused
despite distractions!

Day 36

I keep my energy up no matter what!

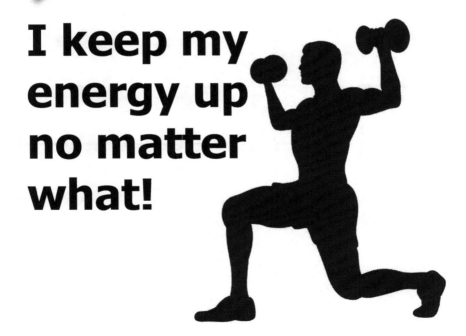

Day 37

I don't dwell on the past

I focus on the now moment and the future!

Day 38

I keep my thoughts on-point today!

Day 39

I am going to kick negativity's butt today!

Day 40

My past does not equate to my future!

Day 41

I take action on what I know I need to do!

Day 42

I don't let negativity take my power!

Day 43

I focus on abundance today!

Day 44

I am inspired to get done what needs to be done today!

Day 45

I don't think it I do it!

Day 46

I prioritize my goals and get them done!

Day 47

Today, I look in the eyes of my pain and say,

"You will not win!"

Day 48

I do not doubt myself!

Day 49

I stay motivated!

Day 50

I do what is brave today!

Day 51

I am going to make today a great day!

Day 52

I will have successful outcomes today!

Day 53

I focus on the outcome I want to happen today!

Day 54

I learn from my mistakes,

and don't do them again!

Day 55

I tackle the tough stuff today!

Day 56

If something is not happening the way I want, **I change it up!**

Day 57

I focus on results!

Day 58

You can control your reaction to anything negative!

Day 59

Don't let negativity use you today!

Day 60

I see positivity all around me!

Day 61

I stay away from anything that disempowers me!

Day 62

I execute my mission today, and no negative thoughts will hold me back!

Day 63

I do today what I put off yesterday!

Day 64

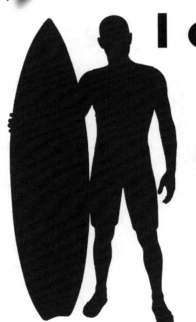

I can handle every challenge!

Day 65

I will help someone achieve their goal today!

Day 66

Change your negative state to a positive state today!

Day 67

I manage my stress rather than my stress managing me!

Day 68

I picture the best outcome for today!

Day 69

I know my power and I use it!

Day 70

I think positively,
Act positively,
And speak positively!

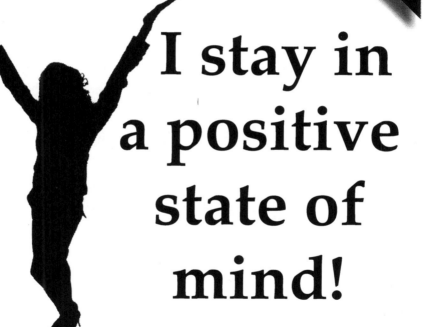

Day 71

I stay in a positive state of mind!

Day 72

I remind myself of all that I have to be thankful for today!

Day 73

I find my power today!

Day 74

I delete my negative thoughts today!

Day 75

I unleash my power!

Day 76

I release any negative emotions today!

Day 77

I look for ways to grow today!

Day 79

I will get through this!

Day 80

I don't depend on others for my happiness!

Day 81

I remember the good things from my past, not the bad!

Day 82

I trust in my abilities today!

Day 83

I don't let my negative past effect my future!

Day 84

What I think today becomes my reality!

Day 85

I remember my purpose today!

Day 86

What I think today becomes my reality!

Day 87

I visualize my success today!

Day 88

I can handle whatever comes my way today!

Day 89

I am going to stay stress-free today!

Day 90

Today, I will not listen to my negative thoughts!

Day 91

I don't let negative emotions control me!

Day 92

I am going to be unstoppable today!

Day 93

I don't listen to procrastination!

Day 94

I say what I want to do, instead of what I have to!

Day 95

I interrupt any negative patterns in my life!

Day 96

I anchor all my thoughts on the positive!

Day 97

I am going to have fun today no matter what happens!

Day 98

I don't allow negativity to wound me!

Day 100

Identify any beliefs that hold me back and don't listen!

Day 101

What I am is bigger than the negative!

Day 102

I don't do anything to sabotage myself or my success!

Day 103

I attract the things that help me today!

Day 104

I have empowering beliefs!

Day 105

I don't let thoughts of the past effect me!

Day 106

I am grateful for all that I have!

Day 107

I attract abundance!

Day 108

My positive attitude is bigger than negative illusions!

Day 109

I work on making my life greater today!

Day 110

I don't limit myself today!

Day 111

I associate with the positive
rather than the negative!

Day 112

I do what I must do!

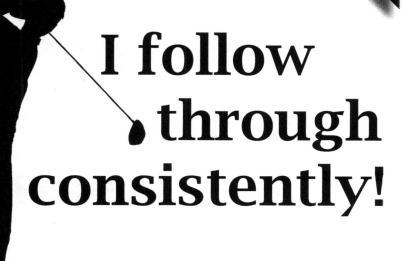

Day 114

I will execute my strategy successfully today!

Day 115

I follow through consistently!

Day 116

I don't let crises mess me up today!

Day 117

I don't let my wounds control me!

Day 118

I manage my stress effectively today!

Day 119

I am bigger than negativity!

Day 120

I am results driven today!

Day 121

I am worthy and ready!

Day 122

I use my heart today!

Day 123

I control my mental focus today!

Day 124

I don't let negativity take control!

Day 125

I know my potential!

Day 126

As soon as negativity happens,
<u>I look for the positive!</u>

Day 127

I take action on my beliefs and see results!

Day 128

I remove thoughts of fear today!

Day 129

I don't let any negativity control my life today!

Day 130

Positivity is my focus today!

Day 131

I give more than I get today!

Day 132

I carry out my positivity strategy today!

Day 133

My life is balanced and peaceful!

Day 135

I define my day;

I don't let my day define me!

Day 136

I don't stress today!

Day 137

I vibrant positivity not negativity!

Day 138

I do not let negativity control my life!

Day 139

I get what I want!

Day 140

I see all my opportunities today!

Day 141

I am flexible!

Day 142

I take an oath of action!

Day 143

I am blessed!

Day 144

I am resourceful!

Day 145

I learn from every experience!

Day 146

I don't let anything shake my confidence!

Day 147

I live each day with power and passion!

Day 149

I build my courage muscle today!

Day 150

Every day I work on the new me!

Day 151

I let go of my mental limitations!

Day 152

I consistently think positive thoughts!

Day 153

I use my personal power to make it happen!

Day 154

I maintain a positive mental state!

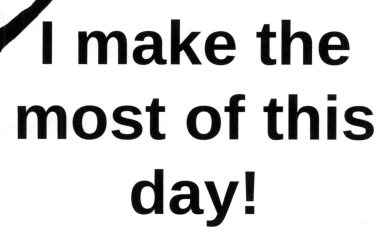

Day 155

I make the most of this day!

Day 156

I am going to focus on my breakthrough!

Day 157

My mission is going to be successfully completed today!

Day 158

I invest in myself today!

Day 159

I keep my energy positive!

Day 160

I experience no fear today!

Day 161

I let no person, place, or thing irritate or annoy me today!

Day 162

I am going to enjoy this day!

Day 163

I will get the victories I want today!

Day 164

My negative thoughts *cannot* hold me back!

Day 165

I will not doubt nor hesitate!

Day 166

I remember my positive thoughts

not my negative ones!

Day 167

I stay in my positive space!

Day 168

I keep my mind in control today!

Day 169

I trust my **power!**

Day 170

I claim a new positive pattern!

Day 171

I have confidence
and courage
no matter
what happens today!

Day 172

I act on my purposeful intention!

Day 173

I meet life with optimism!

Day 174

It's you against you.

Decide to WIN today!

Day 175

Doubt your doubt!

Day 176

Whatever it takes!

Day 177

I use my talent today!

Day 178

I don't let fear stop me!

Day 179

Great things are coming my way today!

Day 180

I can get it done!!

Day 181

Remember who you are today!

Day 182

I ignore mental clutter!

Day 183

I see through the illusion!

Day 184

I remember my power and ability today!

Day 185

I don't let negativity program me!

Day 186

I am positive and fearless!

Day 187

I follow peace today!

Day 188

I am bigger than my problems, concerns, and worries!

Day 189

I am not addicted to worry!

Day 190

I adapt and change!

Day 191

I don't think thoughts of doubt!

Day 192

I am clear, calm, and connected!

Day 193

I have the courage to do what needs to be done today!

Day 194

I face each day with passion!

Day 195

I am not going to be in an emotional prison today!

Day 196

I use my champion spirit to get things done!

Day 197

I talk back to negativity!

Day 198

I manage my emotions instead of my emotions managing me!

Day 199

Don't agree with negativity!

Day 200

I get out of my own way today!

Day 201

I maintain my peace no matter what happens!

Day 202

I don't make choices from ego!

Day 203

I am okay with the outcome, no matter what happens!

Day 204

I accept this challenge!

Day 205

I do not let this worry and fear have power over me!

Day 206

Any *NO* means a "Next Opportunity" is on the way!

Day 207

I don't let negativity overpower me!

Day 208

I am going to get the breakthrough I want!

Day 209

I am bold and brave!

Day 210

I choose only thoughts that strengthen me!

Day 211

I tell negativity no!

Day 212

I will defeat negativity today!

Day 213

Every day my attitude is becoming more positive!

Day 214

I am present to the lessons of my journey today!

Day 215

I will accomplish what I need to do today!

Day 216

Be still and know everything is going to be okay!

Day 217

All my thoughts today are going to be positive!

Day 218

I declare myself free from negativity!

Day 219

I starve my distractions and feed my purpose!

Day 220

I am a positive person!

I find a way!

Day 221

I work toward my mission today!

Day 222

I ask for what I want!

Day 223

I don't let what others think about me hold me back!

Day 224

I don't let negativity win!

Day 225

I am ready to take action!

Day 226

I am a warrior!

Day 227

I can get this done!

Day 228

I attract positivity
not negativity!

Day 229

I don't let negativity beat me!

Day 230

I close my eyes,
breathe slowly,
deeply,
and feel my power!

Day 231

I choose supportive thoughts!

Day 232

I am going to succeed no matter what!

Day 233

I approach my problems in a positive way!

Day 234

I let go of unloving thoughts and unloving emotions!

Day 235

I declare my freedom
from negative thoughts!

Day 236

I don't give energy to negative thoughts!

Day 237

I am enthusiastic!

Day 238

I focus my energy on <u>new thoughts</u>
not old ones!

Day 239

I am amazing & I show it!

Day 240

I do everything with enthusiasm today!

Day 241

I am a get-it-done type of person!

Day 242

I don't let anything take my peace!

Day 243

I release my attachment to negative thoughts!

Day 244

I have a positive and fearless spirit!

Day 245

I choose only positive thoughts!

Day 246

I stay locked in to my mission today!

Day 247

I make the right choices today!

Day 248

I am going to own it today!

Day 249

I find more <u>opportunities</u> then problems today!

Day 250

I don't let negativity separate me from my vision!

Day 251

I let positivity work through me today!

Day 252

I listen to my positive inner guidance!

Day 253

I am positivity's ambassador!

Day 254

Positivity gives me the perfect answer!

Day 255

I let positivity lead me today!

Day 256

I don't focus on the negative!

Day 257

I don't accept negative thoughts about myself!

Day 258

I see the positive in this!

Day 259

I don't accept negative thoughts about myself!

Day 260

I am brave today!

Day 261

Positivity is a lifestyle I am living today!

Day 262

I stay aware of any negative thoughts.

I either:
- delete it,
- transform it,
- or replace it!

Day 263

I see the positive in this!

Day 264

I smile all day today!

Day 265

I let go of the past today!

Day 266

Just because negativity
comes to my mind,
does not mean
I have to let it in!

Day 267

I stop the disease of negativity with positivity!

Day 268

I don't let negativity spread!

Day 269

Don't be loyal to old, invalid belief systems that do not serve you any more!

Day 270

I am going to replace all my negative thoughts today!

Day 271

I use the more powerful me today!

Day 272

I listen to my inner power!

Day 273

I unleash my full potential!

Day 274

I think healthy all day today!

Day 275

I am positivity-centered rather than self-centered!

Day 276

I am going to let my positivity handle *it* today!

Day 277

I do what positivity tells me to do today!

Day 278

I am a positivity enthusiast!

Day 279

I follow positivity's orders today!

Day 280

I think positivity first today!

Day 281

I wear my positivity glasses today!

Day 282

I tap into my positivity today!

Day 283

I release all my negative thoughts!

Day 284

I release
the past!

Day 285

I shed my old negative beliefs!

Day 286

I don't waste my time worrying!

Day 287

I give my best in every moment!

Day 288

I expect the best!

Day 289

I let go of any negativity that runs through my thoughts!

Day 290

I remember to breathe all day!

Day 291

I make positivity my priority!

Day 292

I find my strength and use it today!

Day 293

I look for the positive today!

Day 294

I am going to do what it takes today!

Day 295

I talk and feel from the heart today!

Day 296

I focus on my positive thoughts,

and the best outcome I can envision,

and get myself moving ***to make it happen!***

Day 297

I don't let negativity have any power over me today!

Day 298

I release any conscious or unconscious fears that hold me back from my goals!

Day 299

I am all about positivity today!

Day 300

I open my mind
to the positive outcome
in every situation!

Day 301

Positivity helps with anything that comes my way today!

Day 302

I am all about my goals today!

Day 303

My positive attitude motivates me today!

Day 304

I am positively aligned today!

Day 305

I see the world as positive, not negative!

Day 306

No matter what I have this today!

Day 307

I am absolutely going to make it happen today!

Day 308

Today, I am not going worry!

Day 310

Today,
I am not listening to:
- my pain
- my disappointments
- my past
- or negativity!

Day 311

My positive thoughts nourish me today!

Day 312

I fight negativity **with positivity!**

Day 313

No negative thoughts are going to stop me today!

Day 314

I know I will do this today!

Day 315

I use positive energy to get this done!

Day 316

I can and I will!

Day 317

My positivity guides me today!

Day 318

I use positive self-talk not negative self-talk today!

Day 319

I don't give negativity power!

Day 320

I am going to get results today!

Day 321

I am only one positive thought away from a breakthrough!

Day 322

I defeat negative thoughts with powerful ones!

Day 324

My negative thoughts are only temporary!

Day 325

I think like a champion today!

Day 326

I make all decisions from the perception of my higher self!

Day 327

My positivity is going to get me through this!

Day 328

I learn the lessons I need to learn today!

Day 329

Positivity shapes my day!

Day 330

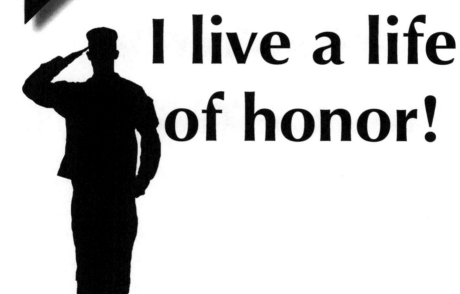

I live a life of honor!

Day 331

A positive attitude today will enhance every experience!

Day 332

I don't let people trigger negativity in me!

Day 333

I make the right choices today, being positive!

Day 334

I attract positive people in my life!

Day 335

Positivity guides my path today!

Day 336

I don't give negative thoughts power!

Day 337

I let nothing break my positive attitude!

Day 338

Everything is going to work out!

Day 339

I am excited about my future!

Day 340

I know a positive mental attitude is the right attitude to have in every situation!

Day 341

I choose positivity instead of negativity!

Day 342

I respond with positivity!

Day 343

I look at the positive side!

Day 344

I have an abundance mentality!

Day 345

I realize a wrong attitude can cause me to focus on the wrong thing!

Day 346

I appreciate the positive things in my life!

Day 347

I am not going to let this problem get to me!

Day 348

I see
amazing miracles
all around me!

Day 349

I use my positive power to get things done!

Day 350

I don't take anything for granted!

Day 351

I am going to have fun with life today!

Day 352

I stay excited!

Day 353

I share my positivity with others!

Day 354

I don't let outside negativity affect my inside positivity!

Day 355

I stay positive!

Day 356

Great miracles are happening in my life!

Day 357

I work on my dream today and get results!

Day 358

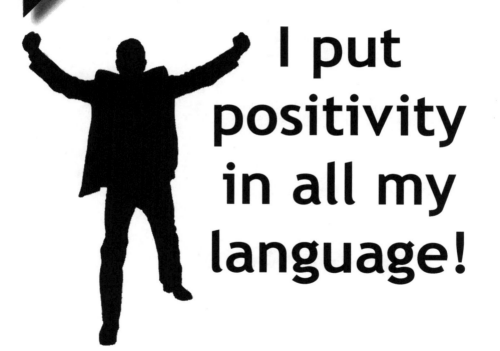

I put positivity in all my language!

Day 359

I am going to get the results I want!

Day 360

People can tell I am a positive person!

Day 361

I focus on the positive!

Day 362

I share my smile with others today!

Day 363

My positive thoughts impact the lives of others!

Day 364

I don't hold onto negative thoughts!

Day 365

I am going to be very productive today!

Made in the USA
Lexington, KY
10 May 2018